After investing her life in teaching and directing, Bronwyn Jardin has such a wise eye and sensitive ear to the world around her: "a vigil of pigeons/ fat and fluffed against the fog/ in their smoky grey coats/watch you from the rooftops." These poems break moments and places into lovely shards of surprise worth our full attention.

–Leslie Leyland Fields, author of *Crossing the Waters* and *The Wonder Years: 40 Women over 40 on Aging, Faith, Beauty and Strength.*

After hearing Bronwyn read one of her poems live at a writers' retreat, I was so happy to have the chance to read more of her work. This collection of poems has not disappointed! Bronwyn has a way of taking me right into the concrete sensations of experiences I've never had. I read *South Florida Salvage* several times in one sitting, soaking in a new phrase each time. I'm stirred and mesmerized.

–Christa Wells, singer and songwriter

Bronwyn Jardin writes poetry that brings together her eye for rich detail, wit, humor, and a certain tenderness. Born from her observations of life in all its *extraordinary ordinary* wonder and delight, her poetry is at once soul-stirring and spirit-calming. She shakes us awake into our own remembering. And brings us along as she explores subjects which are both a bit familiar and uniquely her own, told with a lovely twist. Sitting with her poetry is surely good for the soul.

–Elizabeth Marshall, poet and author

soft trades, hard blows

Soft Trades, Hard Blows

Poems

by

Bronwyn Best Jardin

Love and God's blessings, sweet Mandy! All glory to Jesus for these words!

Bronwyn

For Roy, Seana, Kris, and James

contents

introduction

This has happened because of Mrs. Adams. She published my first "award-winning" poem, "The World is Mine," in the main hall showcase at South Miami Elementary, and from the fourth grade, my future was mapped out. A Godly woman and a whirlwind of creativity, she was a model teacher and I loved her. When I played "school," she was the mentor I mimicked. I didn't know then I would become a teacher and a writer.

But in the early days, writing was one of many horses that raced in my head. Performing onstage lured me constantly, and I discovered wearing a mask hid the nervous child inside. Hence, I spent most of my school years smelling excitement as dusty velveteen stage curtains swept open. Under hot border lights, I could pretend, constantly craving affirmation.

Along with drama, my love of literature and

writing led to a degree in secondary language arts education. For over twenty-five years, changing schools often, thanks to my husband's career, I taught a variety of academic and elective courses from Composition to Technical theatre.

A fellowship in The Northern Virginia Writing Project, at George Mason University, in summer of '93, rocketed me into the writing stratosphere. Suddenly, I craved writing more than food. Small attempts at penning poetry again turned into publication and writing contests. I challenged my high school students to not only think through writing, but to find joy in it.

Eventually, we sunk roots in middle Georgia, and my career took a rewarding return to the stage. Fourteen years as a theatre teacher and director at Houston County High School left little time for writing poetry, plays, or memoirs. After years of collecting the treasures of rigorous one-act play competitions, full length musicals, and many smaller productions, all teeming with incredibly talented young people, I retired from school life.

Here is my new old career. This collection is born from years of journal scribblings, travel diaries, and prayers. First drafts have lighted like butterflies on paper napkins, backs of store receipts, and my hand. Sometimes now, I dictate mumbo-jumbo phrases into my iPhone, while dodging south Florida traffic. Words uncaptured have a pesky habit of fluttering off.

Many understanding and loving people are behind this effort.

Special thanks to Roy, for over four decades, my dearest love, soul mate, and fellow adventurer. It can't be easy living with a writer, but you never complain and keep encouraging me "eight days a week." You speak truth when I hand you those rough drafts and have given me a beautiful space for composing my thoughts. Truly, you complete my life, and together, we know God truly linked our lives!

To Seana, Kris, and James, you have given me love, joy, and inspiration unimaginable as your mom. Each of you and your families are the jewels of my life! Abundant gratitude and kudos to Kris, for many hours of support and playing midwife to the birth of this collection, as well as my website. You have been so lovingly patient through it all!

My dear Carol, you could have easily squashed me as your pain-in-the-neck little sister, but you let me live to grow up. Thank you for being my lifelong, loving "girlfriend" and for urging me to write on.

To my brother-in-law, award-winning artist, Ralph "Rafa," Lopez, who blessed me with my book cover — it's *exactly* what I wanted! I am so honored you shared your gift for this project. Looking forward to more collaboration and more breathtaking watercolor images.

Sarah and Diane, "sisters" who have known me since I was a youngster and put up with my antics, your friendship is so precious to me, and I treasure time we spend "catching up." For decades, you have both nudged me to keep creating, when I wondered if my words could make a difference.

Leslie Leyland Fields's *Harvester Island Wilderness Workshop* '16, *New Smyrna Beach*,'17, and Kris Camealy's *Refine, the Retreat,* '18, gave me the gift of writing fellowship. If I begin to name those of you who encouraged, critiqued, and helped me in those settings, I will likely forget someone, so thank you, my newfound friends. Your talents and faith inspire me.

Christa, Elizabeth, and Leslie, thank you so much for reading some of this book and offering your encouragement, advice, and commendation.

I am honored to know you and am grateful to be a part of your creative world.

So many of you friends and family who have known me for a season or two have been a cheering squad for this endeavor. To each of you who has reached out with notes or prayers, you are much of my reason to put these words together. I offer them as a gift and hope at least one or two pieces will bless your heart.

Special thanks to Pam Lehman for a keen eye and a sharpened pencil with my copy. It couldn't have happened at a busier time for you, and I so appreciate your help, my friend!

I never again saw Mrs. Adams, my first publisher and role-model, but perhaps one day we will meet face to face, and I'll thank her too.

Lastly, and most importantly, thank you Lord Jesus, for your saving grace and for loving me anyway. Every hour, I am nothing without You. All glory is Yours!

carried

I am riding on my father's shoulders.
   My eyes eight feet above sandburs,
   little mouth stretched wide in a squeal
   "Don't drop me!"
   Surely, I am riding an elephant,
   grabbing his red ears.
   He holds me,
   his big hands
   wrapped around my thin shins.
   I am bouncing up here
   now gripping his freckled neck.
   Ducking coconut palm blades,
   salted wind kissing my face,
   we're going to the water!
   He's got me,
   says "I got you,"

won't let me fall.
And he doesn't.
Never did.

forbidden fruit

There were plenty for us to climb,
    our tropical yards amply supplied.
    But each one that we tried
    could not compare with the one
    heavy with hanging fruit,
    whose fragrance sent us high.

    The pine was loftiest of trees,
    Old oak was roughest on our knees.
    The swishing palm...well, shimmying up to his
husky nuts,
    he was too easily done.
    The melaleuca's paper was fun in the stripping,
    'til we left him naked, with no bark of protest.

But the mango! Yes, here was the man.

He welcomed us all—three or four- even more.
Shoulders stooped low, he'd let us in.
How we'd head for heaven in his ample arms!
He took us as we were:
explorers, gypsies, pirates, queens,
and we could hang, sit, stand or lie,
so accommodating was he.

Oh yes, from driveways and porches,
drifted distant protests:
Stay out of that tree!
Don't come crying to me
when you fall on your head, dead!
Keep your feet on the ground!

Ah, but from the ground—
lured up into his
bountiful branches,
itching to touch
his purply-green plums,
scrambling for his highest heights,
not one of us could resist
his sappy song.

Now he took us up
Up, Up! Up!

Breathless
as we went
between grass
And outer space.

Glancing back or
looking up could
make us plunge.
So we took him
one
pound-pounding
heartbeat
at a time,
rising with him,
straddling his branches,
feeling the dance
in the best of breezes,
until we dared go no further up.

And how trembly
was the coming down,
fumbling feet
searching firmest ground.
The forbidden done,
we'd head for home
or play another play;

but all that day
I would know how
we'd touched and tasted
his fragrant fruit,
his tickly traces
of sticky kisses
still prickling
on my arms and legs.

my daylight
mother

Humming your music,
    your black swan hands glided
    across the snowy sheets,
    and my pale ones followed
    like obedient hatchlings.
    We're movin' and smoothin','
    you'd say.

    You tucked inside me
    your workday wisdom:
    Hospital corners
    make a bed look good,
    smooth the surface,
    take all the ripples out.

Together, we plumped up pillows,
floated side by side,
an unmatched pair:
long, ebony woman,
freckled blond girl.

You said, *See, makin' a bed
makes the whole room look right!*
And I listened for your smiles,
watched your laughter sway,
believed your every breath.

As big brown radio
pounded like a heartdrum,
Those working hands
took my little ones,
spun me across shiny floors,
singing Dee Dee's *Mashed Potatoes*,
dancing Chubby Checkers' *Twist*.

We spoke nothing of Rosa and Martin,
backs of busses and Montgomery marches,
while your bony finger pointed
Clean up!
Act nice!

Take pride!

I mimicked your every move,
my daylight mother,
knowing I would never be
just like you
when I grew up.

But I still sing to your memory,
hearing your music,
Movin' and *smoothin,'*
while my hands follow yours
across rippled sheets.

affirmation of life, another bedtime story

Kitchen drawer full of silver
   jangles and slams
   and I, in my stuffy bear room
   fear Mama has finally decided
   to act on her screams
   (perhaps with a paring knife?)
   I shake and crouch
   by the bedroom door,
   straining to hear
   if they are going to fight
   more

Mama?

Mama?
More?

Kitchen chair scrapes across her sobs.
Through a crack, I see her,
head cradled on arms
stretched like pale fish
on the empty table
where we pray and eat.

What's wrong with me,
so hungry to hear more?
Pressing my cheek
on cool smooth wood,
hoping she'll throw scraps
more shouts, more noise,
comforting food,
I swallow in knots,
soothing me to sleep. . .
Shh...she will be there...
shh, she'll still be there
when I wake up in the morning.

manoa campus in
the 'seventies

Standing in a doorway,
  he smiled a wicked hello.
  Fall semester had rolled behind them,
  leaving Crane and Melville in their wake.
  They hadn't known one another well,
  seated at their desks, flirting with mystery,
  studying the treasure map laid before them.
  He knew she had a flyer fiancé.
  She knew he had a house in the valley.
  She'd only been there in her head,
  after never leaving sandals by his bed...

Now he held open a theatre door

and smiled, his lips pressing against silent
wishes
   and they traded pretty little trinket words
   like shy cheeky kisses.
   Then he tilted her sidewalk plank,
   like a sudden eight foot swell,
   when she thought he said something about
   If you weren't getting married, I'd ask you out.

Been through some hard squalls and wild
waters
   with her island pilot and three gypsy hearties. . .
   Now in softer seas and lapping harbor,
   phantoms drift like mist in distant dreams;
   she has never wished for anything more.
   Still, she can see that haole boy's Sunset Beach
hair,
   a crazy crew of reckless freckles
   capturing his tanned pirate face.
   Almost forgot she ran into him in that time, in
that place.

young aloha in
the city

Green apple dreams
   still kiss my lips:
   sweet tangy delicious
   dripping warm afternoons,
   in soft valley rain
   coming down in cool sheets.
   Tasting cold and crisp
   half-a-Granny Smith,
   walking above sidewalks
   breeze drying damp hair
   butterfly feet
   skimming hilly streets
   past tourist busses
   and tire squeak.

Plumeria and smoky diesel
island city of hammering clamor,
I drifted in the savor of you
in late summer,
sleeping and dreaming,
tasting bittersweet fruit,
in trade winds of wandering.

communion

Slice for me, love,
   A piece of your day
   And let's steal away
   To the hollow by the stream.

   Bring warm spice
   Brush with kisses
   Heap upon our whispered wishes
   With the lightest whip of dreams.

   Then share each half
   Our lips begin it
   Feast upon each crumbling minute
   Hunger bursting at the seams.

first baby mornings

"Moo moo, woof woof!
Doodle-oodle-oo . . .
Peep peep peep Peep!
Who-hooo Hoo!"

From dreams I stir,
not a cry does she make.
Our baby girl chirps
as she wiggles awake.

Everyday she wants the book:
animals galore.
Let's look and look!

She points "More!" and "More!"

I squawk -wauk chicken,
low like a cow.
I play piggie and doggie,
rooster and owl.

She can't yet name who lives on those shelves,
but she knows how they chatter amongst
themselves.

incarnation

I witnessed
　　your mother's petals opening around you
　　the day you dawned
　　dusky blue, cloud pink, sunlit by the second,
　　through your indignant squalls.

　　Your rosy brilliance
　　filled up the room,
　　overtook my breath
　　while God's hand servants,
　　absurd in their attempts
　　to be equal to you,
　　bustled and scurried,
　　attending as you made your choice
　　to grace us with your day
　　or return to the realm of unbloomed dark.

Standing in streams of blood and water
shaking like a virgin,
I dared to touch your mother's hand,
felt my knees fail and bowed my head,
bathed in light commanding genuflection.

—

mornings with bright-eyes

Barely awake,
   I creep by on softest feet
   to get down the hall and back
   before she and sister wake.
   Maybe I'll sneak
   just another breath of sleep.
   Eight months spent,
   precious is the rest.

But when I tiptoe past her crib,
   she is standing, leaning, grinning,
   little daisy petal fingers
   spread tight on the rails.
   Hello! her bright eyes shine,

like sunlight stretching arms
out from under wooly grey dawn.
She dances for her drink.

Swayed, I sweep her up into my bare arms,
as she pats my gown,
scrunching roly-poly against my breast.
Covering her bonbon cheeks
and feathery head in sleepy kisses,
I take us to the covers.
Our few quiet minutes. . .
except that she hums and smacks her lips.

We soon ease into the ancient peace,
those golden eyes now shaded by whispery
lashes.
Lying in this cradle of my arm,
her tiny mouth quivers in delicious dreams.
She doesn't yet know what I know
about the racing light rippling through the
curtains
and the speed of the earth in its embrace of the
sun.
More sleep? Maybe soon.

Too soon, as mornings must go,

She'll wake to quick oats and bottled juice,
backpacked, bounding to the bus stop,
too rushed for good-bye kisses.
Besides, it will be science test day.
Her mind will not be on me,
but on matter and light,
on energy and motion.

early morning
before work

Glitter dances on my windshield.
   Firmly wipers whisk away
   (vainly, vainly whisk away)
   Here we go, we're off and inching
   through the foggy morning misting
   lighted bump-to-bump-to- bumper
   dripping silver scarlet shine.

   Here we go, we're up and moving.
   Stop sign knits us close together
   gripping tires are ever sliding,
   ever slowly, ever sliding
   to the office, Monday ready:
   Black on white and click and ring

Gleaming green fluorescent glares.

(vainly, vainly whisk away,
vainly, vainly whisk away)

Why I feel this longing, wrenching,
why I'd rather feel this drenching
(Vainly, vainly whish away,
Vainly, vainly wish away)
only seems a misty puzzle,
not unlike this dancing drizzle.

wild things

Jimmy and our canary, Tweety,
   have so much in common:
   Led by the Great Conductor, they wake
   with the first flash of morning's baton,
   warm up their wind instruments, and burst
forth
   in their daily concerto of joy.
   They scatter their food with wild abandon
   and could not care less `
   where they make a mess.

The essential difference between boy and bird,
   aside from feathers and tousled hair,
   is, of course, that the tiny friend
   is confined to his comfy cage,
   while the wingless wonder

manages to fly all over the whole house
upstairs or down,
leaving a trail of delightful destruction
in his fledgling flight path.

my littlest

A woman who has
   cradled young
   knows within weeks.
   I couldn't carry you
   long enough
   to be certain.
   I would never
   cup your downy head
   in my trembling palm.
   But I dream
   of your tiny soul,
   seeking a tender strand of nest.
   Brief as a catch of breath,
   like a fragile bud of too early spring,
   you bowed your head,
   curled yourself up

rocked to eversleep,
hearing last the hymn of my heart.

A few days later
than I should have been,
my temple walls quaked and shook
as you slipped away from me. . .
Dear little dream,
one day our souls will meet,
after all.
After all these years
I remember you.
Why else would my eyes ache,
pressed tight like a locket,
wondering about
the what – if You?

prestidigitation, after the ninth life

Perhaps Mother isn't sure
    just where Prissy is...
    since yesterday's today
    And winter's spring.
    But we all know,
    sometimes Mother too,
    that Miss Priss sleeps
    deep
    beneath the bottlebrush tree
    in the backyard.

The crystal glass by Mother's bed
Still holds a little water

–imagine that–
A cut-glass tumbler for a sassy cat!

When the water is gone too,
and Mother stuffs her tissues
down in the glass,
I can just see her
waiting for Dad to toss them out
(though she sleeps
most of the day,
leaving a corner
where Prissy sat.)
She'll watch him
whip out one
after another,
as if with scarf magic,
He could conjure the cat!

by design

Like a child's dot-to-dot
   Freed from a color book page.
   They rush over me:
   dark ribbons of them
   streaming across a lavender sky–
   More,
   still more-
   Now white with light
   as far as the horizon.
   Cattle egrets, I think,
   headed for a brown misty field
   churning with crawlers
   fleeing 'cross the furrows,
   scurrying for safety,
   burrowing into earthy basements.
   And I, sure-footed, warm on my run

flock with my damp and determined fellows
streaming around the same block,
homing toward steaming black coffee
And plump dotted berries.

better than a
vanilla day

Better than a vanilla day
    certain things are. . .
    like hurtling down a highway
    eighty-five miles an hour,
    with a steaming cheeseburger
    half-unwrapped on my lap

    Or running into the wind
    cooling the silvering roots of my hair,
    wafting the onion scent of someone's supper,
    as evening serves up flaming peach
    over the Everglades.

    Big black summer storms:

all day builders
flexing their billowy biceps
'til – FLASH! — BAM!
they rumble and boom
the hot breath out of an afternoon!

Bare feet in shorebreak
standing small and still on running sand
Snuggling pink cheeky babies
blowing rainbow bubbles

Frothy hot chocolate
frosty day on a ferris wheel
or swooshing downhill
in icy blue light
of an Alpine pinnacle.

But better still
are uncertain things:
Surprise side trips
losing a map on dappled lanes
an impromptu dance
wandering and lingering
no reservations.

homestead

We found it after,
   battered down, almost buried
   by tangled traitor trees
   who once offered shade.
   Its hush after the storm,
   a howling silence, haunts me still.

   Its eyes once reflected
   light from the sidewalk:
   bicycles, skateboards, cruising cars
   Rolling and riding the easy current.
   Wild parakeets laughed from pattering palms.

   Eyes now vacant, staring, black.

   Untrained detectives, we enter the back

through a gaping wound.
A dwelling dead,
is now dangerous, wrapped in
corkscrew metal, splintered wood.
With boots and rake, we move with care.

Easier to let it go in rotting egg air
Camera rolling, numb narration. . .
detachment keeping hearts in check:
Watch the glass there–
          Get that picture-
Slow through here, we need more light!

We want to know how it lost this fight
Drowning? Slosh through water to our knees.
Beating? Touch the bruises on the walls.
Stabbing? Crunch the daggers underfoot.
Which came first?
When did it go?

Look! The last breath in the house
caught in a bouquet of birthday balloons
above the leaf-decked table.
Mark the time of death
on the frozen face.
of our little Jim's clock.

We'd left it to die alone.

Yet, the bulldozer burial behind us,
Absurdities stir us from our sleep:
Nights, though windless,
we hear a moan.
The roof isn't leaking,
we feel the rain.

We're snug and covered,
but shards dig deep,
down in the dark,
in the vault of our bones.
Is there a heaven for a house that dies?
What becomes of the soul of a home?

south florida salvage

(In loving memory of Art Best)

To portable crackle and squawk
Of AFTER DISASTER radio,
My father's hands lit a hurricane lamp,
made me sit down,
gave me a paper plate. . .
Canned foods he'd warmed on the grill
corned beef hash...green beans
half-smiles of sliced peaches

In the flickering creep of electricless dusk,
breathless heat of his August porch,
tired tears rode the fringe of storm

grinding across the glades of my gut.
I smelled my salty hair
could scarcely swallow
what he called
Strength for Tomorrow

Clinging to fraying ends of community,
battered by squalls of losses and memory
Our House...Home...Homestead...
I sat where I could see him,
fought to take down that food. . .
Nobody could have comforted me more
with such helpless hands,
such candlelit eyes.

cacophony that christmas

Red light.
   ...but I can't stop
   crystalline fragments
   careening, crashing in my head,
   whining like window glass

   Sirens rise out of
   Nightsea of white lights,
   Then flashing blues.
   While I wait for them

   ...in a rearview mirror
   of months and miles
   I see Will in his yard

grinning, toting green
neatly sawed Saturday clippings
clean from trees
bursting tropical voluptuousness.
Joe, young fly boy next door,
mounting his cycle
revving up our engines
all over the neighborhood,
smiling shiny in South Florida sun
and I am on my evening run,
running in my rhythm
racing home to supper,
heart thrumming in my ears,
like summer thunder
chasing me up the walk. . .

Green light
and I drive home on black ice,
(new map tucked between the seats)
tumbling through my tunnel,
trapped in pictures
of a place left for dead

. . .I danced in a club
with blown out walls
I knelt in a church

without a roof
I ran on a path
now buried in brush. . .

Passing faces
of parting neighbors:
Will was speechless,
Fly boy stunned.
In silence deafening
on our shattered street,
we rationed goodbyes
like warm bottled water
in an August hot nightmare
of splintered palm stumps
bloodless car wrecks
cardboard boxes
of all we owned. . .

Crayon brights!
I lurch up my driveway
as Nameless Neighbor's
giddy Christmas lights
shout me a greeting,
chase up his porch,
race across his gutters
plunge into the ground

and I hope they don't
cause a fire in dry leaves
and burn down the block.

'Cause I've had enough calamity.
My bones rattle with cacophony!
I may just sit in this garage
a few minutes darker
before I go inside
where survivors who love me
kill me with their noise.

surviving andrew

Months after,
   Still scrubbing photos,
   I'm stabbed by a reminder.
   Tiny souvenir in my palm:
   slice of glass
   deep
   clear blue
   as the eye of the storm,
   in warm red sea of skin
   whorling around it,
   counter-clockwise

spur through
manassas

In a blink of the chase,
    before shadows stretch long
    and settle for the night,
    I see them gathered:
    four stately stallions
    standing patient at supper.

I would slow my passage,
    offer minutes like apples,
    if not for the home-bent riders
    reining for no one,
    save the fallen,
    when they must.

Though trapped in the race,
I cast out a lasso,
capture their spirits
for dreams before I sleep. . .
gentle beasts without burdens
on their sun-saddled backs.

resting place

The morning we heard you died
   your white attendance card
   trembled in my hand.
   Where was I to put you?
   You were present
   but couldn't shuffle in
   to sit alone by the door.
   You weren't out for the day,
   didn't belong with the absentees...
   You had to rest somewhere.

   So I pressed your name
   tight in my palm
   forever engraving
   the angles of your still smooth face.
   And then, because I couldn't bear

to toss you away or bury you
deep in forgotten clutter
of paper clips and sticky notes,
I laid you gently on top of my desk,
kept vigil while I tried to teach
Tone and Mood...

Three days later carried you home,
tucked in loving ceremony.
In the privacy of my roll book:
You, surrounded by silent columns,
Embraced by a hundred oblivious classmates.

girl near
bubblegum lane

My children went back to school this fall,
    but your autumn came too early,
    slate shadows growing long across
    your parents' sturdy smiles.

I want to go back too,
so much still unlearned
while three times your years
have made me wise.

Too many why's still haunt my days,
when I pass your lane
and recall the piles of leaves
you should be stirring

with shiny brown loafers,
penny lucky;
the jack o' lanterns
you should be impatient to carve
as you skip from one day to another
out of long September
into orange October
and blacker nights.

Faith, not fact, seems the only logic.
I should have grown old and gone first,
after weeping at your wedding,
or at least graduation. . .

This untimely blur of leaves and lilies
lining dark asphalt, along your lane,
makes me burn to understand,
God, please tell me why.

Shall I follow my babies back to the classrooms
for lessons they might teach me?
Or maybe just stand there beside them, loving
their breathing
Just a few seasons longer, a few seasons more.

day after jennifer

Seam
Of sky and river
Unraveled by soothing rain
All day drizzle and fog, like holy water and
incense.
A new sacrament: Revelation unbinds
boundaries
Buries barriers
Heaven and earth   mother and child   seamless
circle
Simple and eternal
as a fingertip of
rain.

before all souls

Sliding into the fall,
  chilled by scalding chocolate,
  too eager for the sweet,
  I see my days like dusty pebbles,
  spill and spatter at my feet.

  Would I could twine afternoon
  slats of light and shadow,
  tucking time in a basket, wide and deep,
  while grayness frays and fades the maples,
  making their colors go to sleep.

  When I fear a cold and early moon
  will eclipse me in the criss-cross
  of day and dusk she weaves,

You embroider my darkness–a sunny mum surprise
blossoming under the heels of slippery brown leaves!

temporality

Steadfast snowman,
   Brave sentinel!
   Your hours are draining down the driveway.
   Next door, a vigil of pigeons,
   fat and fluffed against the fog
   in their smoky grey coats,
   watch you from the rooftop,
   sink where you stand,
   swallowed by soggy ground.

   Cartoon of man,
   as you pass,
   ashes to ashes,
   ice to mush,
   do you wonder, too,
   about the next world?

Perhaps as a puddle?
Or just ooze to oblivion,
to the comfortable crooning
of your surviving mourners?

exit music

In the finale,
    I want to go,
    Not when the world succumbs to snow,
    But when the woods dance sun and flame,
    With a fanfare of leaves
    And cymbal wind blow.

    May I rush down the river
    Fortissimo, free,
    In russet and gold
    To a waiting sea.

    For the notes of my soul
    Should ripple and soar
    Along some crashing splashing shore!
    Let fading forests segue to snow:

In their symphony of silence
The sound of no more.

school grounds

Blanched, severed limbs
   lay drying in the heat.
   Tangled, clawing fingers reached
   for what they could no longer feel:
   whispered beat of mockingbird wings
   heavy curtains of tropical rains
   dewy dawns and simmering sun.
   All pulsed in the river network
   coursing through its veins.

No more.

One of several chores,
in a day's work,
it was felled.
No child I asked seemed to know why.

. . . Don't know why it made me cry.

Days later, between classes
when I passed the sawdust,
I missed the shade.
Someone in the office
tried to teach me:
It had to go. . .
it was an ugly tree
and full of bugs.

to my old friend, whom i can never comfort

I thought about calling,
  wishing I could give you the joy of talky-talk
  like chuckles of a tireless brook.
  Do not mistake my silence for distance.

  When I think of the bitter cliffs you climb,
  the stone you trace with mourning fingers,
  do you know what tremors pass beneath
  the sunny landscape of my face?

  Traveling beside you, I grumble about
  the flight of my living children,
  before I measure the pain

my echoes may cause.

What plummets you must suffer,
when I stumble over my little losses.
How you'd give your blood
To have my pebbles under your feet!

gone with gable

You with the Clark Gable eyes:
   (Yeah, let 'em Google-oogle that one)
   So you saw me first onstage.
   I made you laugh...made you look!
   But you were the matinee idol.
   I would spend a lot of vain years,
   jealous, silly tears
   getting used to sharing
   in your star-space.

   You lit into my place on this planet
   (not sure who knocked whom flat),
   tapped your rhythm on my heartpane
   like some cocky rocker robin,
   caught me crashing against
   my quiet cage walls,

freed me to fly
with your busy beautiful man hands,
while booming the accelerator
of your blurring blue Bug
and my whispery little heart.

This skin's been feeling your driven rhythm
most of my days on this rock,
backed up by island chants, ka-chunk-a-chunka
strums
swinging slack-key and knockin-hard gourds.
...You, dancing our giggling babies in your arms
across the living room floor,
your fingers poppin-boppin off
anything standing still beside you.
Your snapping fire has so often
warmed my weariness.

But the thing is,
The real thing is, you.
(Moving me, shaking me
Sleeping and waking me),
I look in your eyes
and there's the flash that fuels me fast:
when right needs uprighting
And the ground needs standing,

your cadence thunders like a rumbling drum
line
  with a blaze that roars up a burst of stars,
  keeping the wild back by the woods.
  The thing still catching my breath is,
  frankly, Gable eyes,
  you do give a damn.

everybody has one

Black cats
  Mice
  Men from Mars
  Falling
  Flying
  Rushing cars
  Darkness
  Closets
  Open air
  Heights
  Depths
  Winding stairs
  Foreign places
  Stuffy spaces

Spiders
Lizards
Thunder
Wind
Strangers
Snakes
Haunted yards
Me alone
in Christmas cards

kairos*

Still trembling,
   awestruck his new brother – friend
   warmed his shoulder
   with a gentle hand
   (perhaps like a father he has never known),
   he pries open the smooth card
   with a dark crusty thumbnail.
   He glances at the guard, then reads.
   Words he has never felt
   embrace his hardened palms:
   Jesus loves you and so do I.
   . . .praying for you,
   as you begin this journey
   . . .knowing Him better. . .
   Never read
   never seen

never heard
He cannot continue.
The ink handwriting is bleeding into
tiny puddles, swirls of blue melting
neatly printed *loves* and *you*.
He tries to stop losing the words,
bending his body,
pressing his knotty hands against
his scarred face, trying in vain
to hide the tear tattoo under his
blind eye.
But like a tattered picket fence,
his old fingers fail to stop the flood.
So he closes the card,
staring at the sunrise photo on the front.
He cannot look at all this light
all at once.
Maybe later
he will try again.
He feels the sliding weight of falling chains,
knows with this blinding dawn,
he will never be the same.

*Dedicated to the men and women who offer their time,
resources, and prayers for Kairos prison ministry, giving love

and hope to the forgotten ones, to the glory of the Savior Jesus
Christ.)

pele's tears

Locals say they rain down
   with the lava explosion
   bursting furious from Kilauea.
   The goddess, they believe,
   roars like doomsday, blasts her fireblood tears
   up into the smoky cold
   and they spatter hard,
   icy black
   tiny,
   twisted
   or perfect pearls.

Does she cry from anger?
Has she been betrayed
by the ones who should have loved her,
treasured her sloping frame?

Or does she weep for so many years of holding
back,
  keeping quiet her simmering secrets?

All I know is what I saw beside my tired feet
on dark tunneled rock.
There, among shiny, scattered stones,
a tiny tip of finger pried away the burnt blanket.
a determined, grasping green fern pushing,
pulling up, surely whispering to the Creator:
I refuse.
I will not bow
beneath this seismic crush!

These are my island treasures:
Pele's gem in a little black box
lined in bridal white satin
never lets me forget
unstoppable life,
reaching through the ashes,
raised out of the rock
by a shower of tears.

continuing
conversation

Oh, Father,
   It's me again
   Head hanging low.
   Where did you go?
   . . . No,
   sinking fast in my self-made mush,
   Where did I go?
   Why the same show?

   You, who spun out the stars
   Sculpted every rose
   Honed every bone
   Never left me alone.
   No.

But I drowned like a stone
chose blind, played deaf.
Then you breathed me up,
revived with bread, shared your cup.

Oh Lord, my God,
You embrace my weary soul
raise up tired eyes
toward sun-spired skies.
Yes,
Your hands hold my time.
Your ways have no why.
Up from deep, I fly, I fly!

threads

Tears unravel my waking.
  First, the prick of a needle of memory.
  A silvery crystal thread travels
  across the ruddy fabric of my face.
  But, once done,
  God's fingertip brushes over it,
  quieter than a whisper.
  He smooths and soothes
  his handiwork,
  the stings and the solace.
  I am repaired,
  tenderly sewn new,
  Each morning made new.

wildflowers

Your breath is soft on my neck,
like ground wind whispering to wild wisteria,
and I am swayed.
We dance.
and like an evening primrose,
I wrap up for the night,
curling beside you, small and tight,
and dream big bluebonnet skies
sweet mockingbird music
rising goldenrod.
I wear only Queen Anne's Lace,
flourished by angel trumpets.
I am gathered in your eager arms,
your warm lips near my ear,
waking every wisp of my autumn hair.

under the soft
pine

Sweet Florida breath of Fall
    brings a pine needle here and there
    floating down, from wispy green
    down, down to join
    a soft brown mat
    where I too could lie.

    I don't think the needle minds
    when its time is done.
    It goes the way of all pine:
    evergreen for appointed seasons
    then letting go of sticky hands,
    resting silent at my feet.

Perhaps I won't mind either,
in a soft November breeze,
slipping down the low hanging bough
and resting in the embrace of warm earth
and springing up one day,
up and over the tallest tree,
far above the gulf and glades
beyond every galaxy

on nani kai pond

Light draws me out of shadowy little death,
tugs, pulls me out of dreaming,
picking away sticky strands of slumber
spun by devils once disguised,
now lurking, leering, never leaving me alone.

Light leads me to the blind
where I will see Nani Kai,
though her face may be still,
untroubled yet by waking wind
and circles stirred by snake birds and black-
bellied ducks.

She bids me open my eyes,
leave spidery dreams in twisted sheets.

Come see! she calls,
holding up her mirror,
Behold, see the water gleam!
Look above and below your drowsy head!
Before the turtles and tadpoles crack the glass
before the herons and cranes and fishes come
dancing on the drafts of day,
Open your eyes!

   Swooping terns, like black-capped sisters in
white
   arrive with winged brooms, sweeping away lazy
mist,
   their welcome unveiled every new dawn:
   On Nani Kai's face is the infinite space
   the Father of peace and grace calls Home.

postscript

Unblinded survivor of storms,
   I walk now in any wind:
   fists in my face or breeze at my back.

   And looking up, accept baptismal rain,
   stopping often by muddy roadsides
   to return the smiling gaze of black-eyed Susans.

Made in the USA
Columbia, SC
12 February 2019